ALL AROUND THE WORLD
ESTONIA

by Kristine Spanier, MLIS

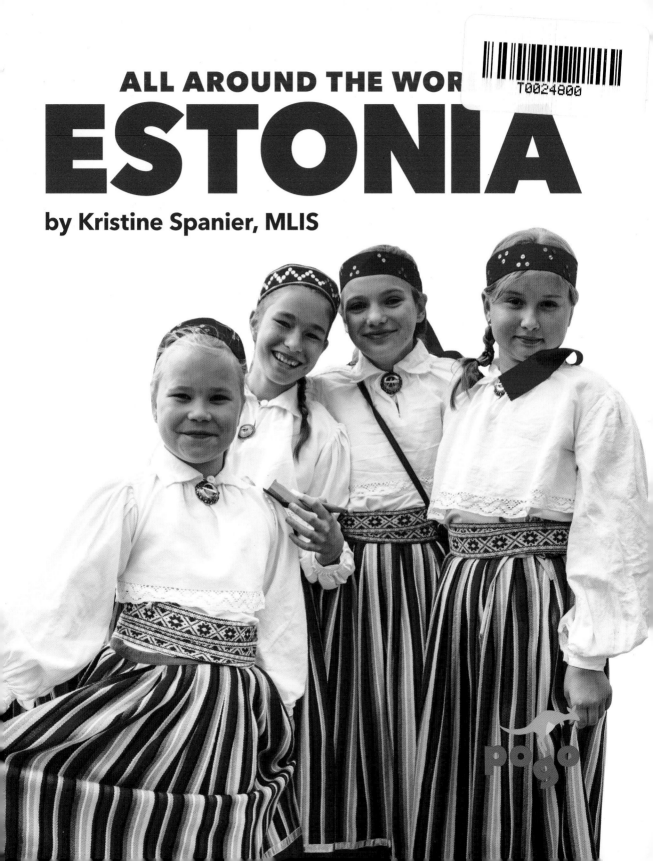

Ideas for Parents and Teachers

Pogo Books let children practice reading informational text while introducing them to nonfiction features such as headings, labels, sidebars, maps, and diagrams, as well as a table of contents, glossary, and index.

Carefully leveled text with a strong photo match offers early fluent readers the support they need to succeed.

Before Reading

- "Walk" through the book and point out the various nonfiction features. Ask the student what purpose each feature serves.
- Look at the glossary together. Read and discuss the words.

Read the Book

- Have the child read the book independently.
- Invite him or her to list questions that arise from reading.

After Reading

- Discuss the child's questions. Talk about how he or she might find answers to those questions.
- Prompt the child to think more. Ask: How does the change of seasons affect how people spend their time in Estonia? Do you do different activities in different seasons?

Pogo Books are published by Jump!
5357 Penn Avenue South
Minneapolis, MN 55419
www.jumplibrary.com

Library of Congress Cataloging-in-Publication Data

Names: Spanier, Kristine, author.
Title: Estonia / by Kristine Spanier, MLIS.
Description: Minneapolis, MN: Jump!, Inc., [2023]
Series: All around the world | Includes index.
Audience: Ages 7-10
Identifiers: LCCN 2022023578 (print)
LCCN 2022023579 (ebook)
ISBN 9798885241977 (hardcover)
ISBN 9798885241984 (paperback)
ISBN 9798885241991 (ebook)
Subjects: LCSH: Estonia—Juvenile literature.
Classification: LCC DK503.23 .S63 2022 (print)
LCC DK503.23 (ebook)
DDC 947.98—dc23/eng/20220518
LC record available at https://lccn.loc.gov/2022023578
LC ebook record available at https://lccn.loc.gov/2022023579

Editor: Jenna Gleisner
Designer: Molly Ballanger

Photo Credits: scanrail/iStock, cover; Ludovic Farine/Shutterstock, 1; Pixfiction/Shutterstock, 3; Mikhail Markovskiy/Shutterstock, 4; photovideoworld/Shutterstock, 5; TheModernCanvas/Shutterstock, 6-7; Aleksey Fefelov/Shutterstock, 8-9tl; Erik Mandre/Shutterstock, 8-9tr; Vaclav Matous/Shutterstock, 8-9bl; Piotr Krzeslak/Shutterstock, 8-9br; REUTERS/Alamy, 10, 18-19; Rusel1981/Dreamstime, 11; RAIGO PAJULA/AFP/Getty, 12-13; STEPHANE DE SAKUTIN/AFP/Getty, 14-15; Sergii Koval/Shutterstock, 16 (porridge); Fanfo/Shutterstock, 16 (sandwich); salihhov/Shutterstock, 17; Sergei Stepanov/Xinhua/Alamy, 20-21; RomanR/Shutterstock, 23.

Printed in the United States of America at Corporate Graphics in North Mankato, Minnesota.

TABLE OF CONTENTS

CHAPTER 1

BY THE BALTIC SEA

Welcome to Estonia! Would you like to explore a **medieval** city? Many buildings in Tallinn were built in the 1200s. St. Olaf's Church rises above them.

Tallinn

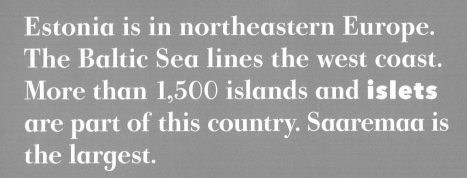

Saaremaa

Estonia is in northeastern Europe. The Baltic Sea lines the west coast. More than 1,500 islands and **islets** are part of this country. Saaremaa is the largest.

hay

Summers are mild. **Crops** grow well. Farmers grow potatoes, barley, and hay. They raise cattle and pigs.

Eight kinds of woodpeckers nest here. The gray-headed woodpecker is one. Brown bears and lynx prowl the forests. Elk and roe deer make homes in them, too.

DID YOU KNOW?

Almost half the land here is forest. Some trees are cut down. The wood is used to make paper, furniture, and other products.

gray-headed woodpecker

brown bear

lynx

roe deer

CHAPTER 2

FREE COUNTRY

Estonians can vote in national **elections** at age 18. They vote for the Riigikogu. Members of this group make laws.

ballot

The Riigikogu meets in Toompea Castle. It is in Tallinn, the **capital**. The Riigikogu elects the president. This is the head of state. The president works with leaders of other countries. The president chooses the prime minister. This person leads the government.

Toompea Castle

The **Soviet Union** formed in 1922. In 1940, it took control of Estonia. People of Estonia **protested**. They wanted their own government. Estonia became **independent** in 1991. The Soviet Union broke apart later that year.

WHAT DO YOU THINK?

During Soviet rule, Estonia's flag was banned. It is now a **symbol** of national pride. Do you think it is important to be proud of your country? Why or why not?

In 2004, Estonia joined the **North Atlantic Treaty Organization (NATO)**. It joined the **European Union (EU)** the same year. Why? These groups help protect countries' freedom. How? The leaders work together.

EU meeting

TAKE A LOOK!

As of October 2022, 27 countries were part of the European Union. Which countries are they? When did they join? Take a look!

YEAR COUNTRY JOINED THE EU

- 1957
- 1973
- 1981
- 1986
- 1995
- 2004
- 2007
- 2013

CHAPTER 3

DAILY LIFE

Would you like to try potato porridge? This is a **traditional** dish. Fish is a part of many meals. Why? There is so much water here!

spiced sprat sandwich

potato porridge

Students learn two languages besides Estonian. Most choose between English, German, Russian, Finnish, and French. After ninth grade, they go to secondary school. They prepare for college or jobs.

In winter, some people watch dogsled races in Otepää. Others explore on snowmobiles.

In summer, some sail on the lakes. Others head out to sea. Visitors enjoy the beaches.

Jaanipäev is June 24. The sun sets for only a few hours. People stay awake all night. They gather around bonfires. They dance and sing.

Estonia is a fun country. Would you like to visit?

WHAT DO YOU THINK?

The Baltica Folk Festival is in summer. People from Estonia, Latvia, and Lithuania celebrate. Countries take turns hosting. People sing, dance, and go to parades. Do you think it is important for people from different countries to get along? Why or why not?

QUICK FACTS & TOOLS

ESTONIA

Location: northeastern Europe

Size: 17,463 square miles
(45,228 square kilometers)

Population: 1,211,524
(2022 estimate)

Capital: Tallinn

Type of Government:
parliamentary republic

Languages: Estonian (official),
Russian, Ukrainian

Exports: wireless network gear,
wind generators, coal tar oil,
refined petroleum, cars

Currency: euro

capital: A city where government leaders meet.

crops: Plants grown for food.

elections: Organized acts of choosing someone or deciding something by voting.

European Union (EU): A group of European countries that have joined together to encourage economic and political cooperation.

independent: Free from a controlling authority.

islets: Very small islands.

medieval: Of or having to do with the Middle Ages, the period of history between approximately 1000 and 1450 CE.

North Atlantic Treaty Organization (NATO): An organization of countries that have agreed to give each other military help. This group includes the United States, Canada, and some countries in Europe.

protested: Demonstrated against something.

Soviet Union: A former country of 15 republics that included Russia, Ukraine, and other nations of eastern Europe and northern Asia.

symbol: An object or design that stands for, suggests, or represents something else.

traditional: Having to do with the customs, beliefs, or activities that are handed down from one generation to the next.

Estonia's currency

INDEX

TO LEARN MORE

Finding more information is as easy as 1, 2, 3.

❶ Go to www.factsurfer.com

❷ Enter "Estonia" into the search box.

❸ Choose your book to see a list of websites.

FACT
SURFER